The 21 Day Happiness Challenge

Learn How to Love Life and Become a Happier Person

by
Olivia S. Taylor

Contents

Introduction   1

Day 1   3
Happiness is...

Day 2   5
Allow yourself to be happy

Day 3   7
Happiness in the brain

Day 4   10
Know thyself

Day 5   12
The corrosive effects of complaining

Day 6   14
The power of gratitude

Day 7   17
The first love of your life - yourself

Day 8   19
Reflection

Day 9   21
Don't take anything personally

Day 10   23
Your external environment

Day 11   26
Practice forgiveness

Day 12   28
Play!

Day 13   31
Inviting stillness into your life

Day 14   33
Give what you want to receive

Day 15   35
More reflection

Day 16   36
Accepting yourself

Day 17   38
Get out of your comfort zone

Day 18   40
Learning to reframe

Day 19   41
Live in the present - intelligently

Day 20   44
Challenge your negative thoughts and beliefs

Day 21   46
Happiness is letting go

Conclusion   49

Other 21-Day Challenges you may enjoy!   50

Introduction

W*hat is happiness?*

Clearly, happiness doesn't have much to do with money, with achievement or with possessions, because plenty of people have all three and are still not happy. In this guide, we'll approach happiness not as something you *have*, but something you actively *do*, each and every day.

Happiness is mysterious, hard to define. A "you know it when you see it" kind of thing. But in many ways, it's also quite simple and straightforward:

- Happiness is a habit.

- Happiness is daily action.

- Happiness is a state of mind.

- Happiness is a choice.

- Happiness is a lifestyle.

True happiness is an "inside job". Look at a happy person's life and you don't see any magic or unicorns. There's nothing in them that isn't also in you. Though external realities can certainly play a role, happiness doesn't spring from what you have, what happens to you, the situation you are in, where you are, or anything else.

In fact, if it was easy to be happy, this book would be a very short one. I could say "decide to be happy" and then you would decide to be happy and that would be the end of it. The irony is that even though we all want happiness quite badly, we lack the skill, consistency and dedication to make happiness a reality ...not "one day", but today, and *every* day.

We look for grand miracles, overnight magic that will take all our problems away, a knight in shining armor or an angel to come and redeem us and give us permission to be content with life. We wait for happiness to be given to us. We resent having to work hard at it.

This may not be the most popular of opinions, but happiness isn't to be found in miracles, or love story happy endings, or winning the lottery, or God himself waving his wand and making everything OK. It comes from you and nobody else, and it happens *now*, not in the past and not in the future.

Day 1

Happiness is...

For some reason, it's easier to answer the question, "are you happy?" than it is to try and define what happiness is in the first place.

Unfortunately, many of us merely substitute in whatever's fashionable at the time - happiness means what our peer group says it does, or our church, or celebrities, or the politics of our particular country in our particular era, or the millions of corporations around us that want to convince us that they too know what happiness is ...and can sell it to you for a price.

Happiness can be the feeling that you're doing "right", that your body is strong and healthy, that you have new experiences and sensations, that you succeed at the goals you set for yourself, that you have the things you want ... or it can simply mean that you are not unhappy.

We'll explore this a little more in Day 4, where you'll start to explore what specifically makes you happy. But today, take a little time to think about happiness itself. Philosophers have wrangled this question for centuries, so you probably won't come to any grand conclusions in just a day. But ask anyway. To get you started, here are some statements about what people over the ages have considered to be "happiness". Which resonate with you right now?

Happiness is...

- Success. Working hard and being good at what you do.

- Living according to a destiny and life purpose.

- Can't be explained - only experienced.

- Being healthy in body and mind.

- A cognitive habit - and something to learn and work at with discipline.

- Love.

- Challenging yourself, embracing fears and doubts and overcoming obstacles.

- Sensations, bliss, transcendent ecstasy - think intoxication, lovemaking, music.

- Unique for each person.

- Ease, luxury, the refined things in life.

- Living a moral and ethical life.

- The joy of creating.

- A social thing to share with others.

- Self expression.

- Something you never really reach, only strive for.

- Laughing at the absurdity of life.

- Overrated.

- Being content, at peace and filled with acceptance.

- Fitness to purpose and doing your best giving your limits.

Today's exercise: what is happiness according to you?

Day 2

Allow yourself to be happy

Perhaps you're a bit like me. You love the idea of committing to being happier, you're ready to do what it takes, and you're going to give it your best... just as soon as you get past this busy week at work. Just as soon as you lose a kilo or two, then you'll be happy. Then everything will be fine. You just need to get to the end of the month / move / get rid of your cold / get that raise, *then* you'll be able to be happy.

Postponing your own happiness can be a bad habit, and what makes it tricky is that you might not even notice yourself doing it. You can imagine yourself happier, more content and with greater well-being ...but that point always seems to be somewhere in the future. In between you and that glorious end goal? All of life's little niggles. All those things you need to clear away. So you see your happiness, sitting just there over the horizon. The funny thing is, the moment you remove those little obstacles, *more* pop up.

You may get frustrated and point to the obstacle. You may say, "If only the kids would just move out, then I could devote more attention to being happy" or "just as soon as I get my bonus, then things will be better" or "when I meet someone special I can really start living life again."

But you deserve to be happy now. Yes, right now.

You don't need to wait until you're prettier / richer / more successful to be happy. Because those goalposts are always moving. You'll end up on your deathbed, thinking, "just as soon as I get into heaven, then everything will be OK."

Right now you inhabit a moment that has the potential to be perfect. For some of us, that prospect is pretty frightening. We may not admit it to ourselves, but putting happiness just out of reach is a way of self-sabotage, a way to avoid making the commitment to your own happiness. It's so much easier to just say, "yes, yes, happiness sounds great ...later".

If you recognize yourself in this, it can be incredibly sobering to admit it to yourself. Look out for sentences that begin with "if only..." or "just as soon as". These are clues that you are unconsciously putting the prospect of happiness out of your reach.

A good question to ask is, why do you feel like you don't deserve happiness?

Today's exercise is to meditate on this and see if you can gently unearth some ways you might be unconsciously holding yourself back from a fuller, happier life.

Day 3

Happiness in the brain

L et's start with some science, shall we? Though we are discovering new things everyday, psychiatrists and neurologists now have a sophisticated understanding of how certain brain chemicals map onto certain emotional states. If you're interested in boosting your feelings of happiness, a good place to start is inside the brain.

To start with, **dopamine** is one of the most well-known. Dopamine is the "reward molecule" and fills your brain with pleasure. Without enough dopamine in your life, you suffer low motivation, inhibition, procrastination ... even full blown clinical depression. Enhance your body's natural ability to be happy and well by giving yourself ample opportunity for rewards.

Break tasks down into small goals so that you feel a sense of accomplishment at each step. Frequently praise yourself for goals you've already achieved, and practice being grateful so you remind yourself of all the pleasurable things already in your life. Give yourself a challenge and you'll feel a rush of dopamine when you solve it. Do something new and exciting, learn a new skill or try a new sensation.

Next up is **oxytocin**, appropriately called the "cuddle hormone" and it's about as lovely as it sounds. Human beings are mammals. Starting in infancy, we all instinctively understand the value of intimacy, of physical closeness - and our brains reward this kind of behavior by flooding our brains with oxytocin.

After childbirth, a new mother's body gets a boost of oxytocin to encourage the bonding process, and we've all experienced a similar boost when we fall in love or experience orgasm. Making sure there's more happy-making oxytocin in your life is easy: cuddle! Even non-physical "cuddling" counts. Spend time with those you love. Socialize. Make love and flirt and snuggle with your partner. Hug. Even cuddling a pet helps (being a mammal too, your pet is most likely down for some extra oxytocin as well). Make room for more skin-to-skin contact, for closeness and kind words, for social bonding.

Serotonin is another neurotransmitter and plays a complicated role in regulating feelings of happiness. Good moods, confidence and wellbeing all arise from having healthy serotonin levels. Up your serotonin levels by practicing positive self-talk, doing affirmations or going into nature regularly.

Endorphins are most commonly associated with exercise, and this is because your body releases them to ease pain and discomfort. Push yourself physically, be a little adventurous and endorphins will be there, giving you that thrilled feeling of accomplishment. Naturally, orgasms are also associated with endorphin release, but obviously, I don't need to tell you that orgasms make people happy.

It isn't all sunshine and rainbows though. "Negative" hormones and neuro-chemicals are also a reality. **Adrenaline** is a hormone that jolts your body into action and prepares you to deal with stress. But if that stress is ongoing, too much adrenaline can be damaging and lead to exhaustion and fatigue. Another stress hormone is **cortisol**, which, when chronically raised, undermines the immune system and dampens your mood.

Taking care of your brain is not much different from taking care of your body in general. A relaxed and well nourished brain will find being happy much easier. Be aware though that hormonal imbalances and subsequently your mood can also be affected by internal factors such as puberty, PMS, menopause or metabolic and hormonal diseases.

Today, your exercise is to make sure you're giving your brain the right physiological support it needs to be happy. Make sure you sleep well, minimize stress, eat a balanced diet high in nutrients and see how you can increase the feel good hormones on a daily base.

Day 4

Know thyself

It seems like such a basic question - *what makes you happy?*

Life can be so crammed full of expectations and obligations and rules and regulations that you may find yourself shocked when you actually stop to ask yourself, "is this even making me happy right now?"

I know that fashion magazines will tell you to take up yoga or go have a walk on the beach to be happier - and these things certainly make some people in the world really happy - but does it make *you* happy?

Today's task is simple. If you want to be happier, it makes sense to include more things in your life that make you happy and fewer things that don't. So, if you have a journal, quickly draw up a list of things that lift your mood.

Be careful though: choose things that *truly* make you happy, not what's "supposed" to make you happy. If watching embarrassing reruns or knitting scarves you'll never wear makes you happy, go ahead and do it. If signing up for a meditation class was boring and uninspiring the last time you tried it, relax, you don't have to try it again now.

Dance, sing, make art, read a book (or write one!), get a massage or take a hot bath, play with your pet, your kids or both, spend time with friends and family (the ones you like, anyway), go out into nature, make love, tinker in your garden, spring-clean the house, do yoga or take a class, bake something, watch a good movie or even indulge in some reasonable retail therapy and buy yourself a little treat.

On the other side of the list, write down things that sap and drain your energy: wasting time on Facebook comparing yourself to others, stressing about your weight, constantly engaging with people you don't like or don't respect you, taking on too much work, or procrastinating on the work you should be doing, stressing about money or debt, having pointless arguments, going to events you don't care about...

Can you make changes to incorporate more of the former and lessen the latter in your life?

A note about addiction: I say "do what makes you happy" but perhaps I should make an exception for, I don't know, heroin. Stuffing yourself with food, binge-drinking, going on a shopping splurge or smoking may make you "happy" ...but not for long. Be realistic about whether something truly adds to your sense of contentment, or whether it's just numbing pain and over stimulating your senses.

<h1 style="text-align:center">Day 5</h1>

The corrosive effects of complaining

There are many ways to sap the joy out of life, to become ungrateful, and to poison your state of mind and the state of mind of those around you. One of the most effective ways? *Complaining*.

I can almost hear you thinking, "complaining doesn't really do anything though - I'm just letting off steam". It's true, one complaint every now and then doesn't matter. But complaining every day? Making a habit of complaining? That *does* do something, and it's dangerous because you might not immediately see the effects.

When you complain, you are sending a clear message out into the world, to others and more importantly, to yourself. You are saying: "This isn't good enough. This is wrong". Not only are you looking at reality itself and turning up your nose, you're communicating a more subtle, more damaging message at the same time. You are telling yourself that life sucks, and nothing can be done about it.

You rob yourself of your own agency in that moment. You shut yourself off to any creative solution, to any fresh perspective, to any humor, when you complain. You say all at once that all of life's great glories and mysteries are not impressing you very much and what's more - you can't be bothered to do anything about it.

Complaining can be such a bummer that it puts the people around you in the same frame of mind. They think, "this person can't be pleased" and unconsciously, they stop trying to please you. When you announce that you are not engaging or communicating anymore with a problem, those around you shut down too. Many times, your complaints about something actually become a self-fulfilling prophecy.

Today's exercise is to make it through the day without complaining! Make a game of it and ask a friend to help you and do the same. If you catch yourself about to do it, challenge yourself by asking:

- Is it really that bad or am I exaggerating?

- What can I do to make this situation better?

- Is there something good in this moment that I am failing to notice?

Get in this simple habit and you'll notice how toxic complaining can really be.

Day 6

The power of gratitude

In many ways, gratitude is like the opposite of complaining.

When you complain, your mind is tuned onto lack, onto what is wrong, onto what you don't have. It's negative by its very definition. The more you do it, the more you're convinced the world is a terrible, sad and disappointing place. Then you can complain even more.

But when we have gratitude, things are different. Our minds are turned onto goodness, positivity and what we already have, not what we lack. When you are receptive to the blessings your life already contains, something strange happens - you begin to notice more and more of them. Then you complain less.

I know that gratitude for the abundance of life sounds like wooh wooh nonsense but in fact, regularly taking time to be grateful has real, measurable effects on your life and sense of well-being. According to a now-famous University of Berkeley study, practicing gratitude changes your outlook in a big way.

How can you take advantage of this?

A gratitude journal is an easy and actually pretty fun way to keep your attention trained on what's important in life: all the beautiful, exciting and wonderful things that surround you day to day but which you may have forgotten to appreciate.

Today's exercise is to start keeping a gratitude journal or to include "gratitude lists" in your regular journal. I like to do a list each morning of 5 items that I'm grateful for. Sometimes the items on this list are big, like being grateful for my loving partner, for my family or for the luck and opportunities that have come my way in life. Sometimes they are just "small" things like the fact that the sunlight coming through the window is particularly beautiful that day, or that I'm having my favorite food for dinner, or that I have legs that can take me wherever I want to go.

Try it for yourself. You'd be amazed at how simply orienting to what's already good in your life can alter your mood and keep your outlook more positive.

Things you could be grateful for today, right now:

- Your body. Can it move, sing, dance, stretch, run and love?

- The people in your life that love you, or those that you love.

- Your favorite music, beautiful art or anything or anyone that inspires that joyful, creative spirit in you - isn't it amazing what human beings can create when they're inspired?

- Take a moment to enjoy the comforts in life. You have a warm bed, good food, the feeling of sunlight on your face, the sound of birds, fresh air and, if you're like me, wine.

- Be grateful for how far you've come in life. Take a moment to appreciate all the lessons you've learned, and all the skills you've acquired.

- Be grateful that you have a life ahead of you, no matter what has happened in the past.

- Be grateful you live in the modern world, that you have access to Netflix and the internet and amazing technologies that let you do amazing things.

No matter what happens today - you have another chance tomorrow to be better. This is a *huge* thing to be grateful for.

Day 7

The first love of your life - yourself

F orgive the corny headline, but it's true.

Many people would do anything for their children or spouses, and yet can't summon up the effort to take themselves to the doctor or treat themselves to a break every now and then. An unhealthy body means an unhealthy mind. Since you are the owner of this body you live in, and since you only get one, it's your responsibility to take good care of it.

Today, think about what you are doing each day that *nourishes* you. You obviously have lots of things in your daily schedule that take away from you, but do you have enough things that are giving back? In other words, are you taking good care of yourself and your body, each and every day?

It's very common these days that somebody neglects their health, pushes themselves past their personal breaking points, doesn't get enough sleep, stresses too much and eats poorly. Your body will go a long way to support you and will suffer silently for quit some time, but when it gets sick, those same people might start wondering what they did to deserve the bad luck, and start to hate their bodies even more.

Sad when you think about it.

Self-care is not something extra or optional in life, it's not about vanity either. A body that is well cared for will last you for a long time, helping protect you from disease and injury, keeping you happy and able to do what you need to. Maintaining the health and wellness of your body means you save money, time and trouble for yourself later on. It's the smart thing to do.

Today's exercise is to think of 3 things you can do right now that will support and nourish this marvelous thing called your body. This could be anything:

- Set aside some time for a proper, full night's sleep. Remove all distractions, make sure your bed is comfortable, the room dark and quiet and allow yourself to wake naturally in the morning.

- Splash out on some delicious, good quality, wholesome food. You're worth it.

- Take a long, head-clearing, stress-relieving walk in a pretty park or somewhere you like. Go with a friend for a chat or bring some poetry.

- Decide to spend quality time with someone you usually put off seeing. Play with your children, have a romantic dinner with your partner or have a chat with a friend you haven't seen in a while. Don't rush, just be in the moment.

- Book a spa treatment like a facial, manicure or massage. Forget about work or family problems and immerse yourself in the moment. Touch can be incredibly healing. Looking fabulous helps too!

- Spend some time doing hobbies you love. Go to a market, be creative, make music, play a game, sport, etc.

- Drink plenty of water, go all out at the gym, have a long soak in the tub or if you have very little time, just do a few moments of deep stretching at your desk: you'll feel better for sure.

Day 8

Reflection

It's easy to read things. It's easy to "know" things. Someone says to you, "you should take better care of yourself" and you think, "yes, yes I know that already" but in fact nothing changes. Why? *Because knowing is not the same as experiencing.*

As we round up to our first week, it's a good time to stop for a bit and have a look at what we've done so far. If you've read through everything without trying the exercises, or tried the exercises half-heartedly and fully intending to fail before you even began, well ... your results may not be that impressive.

On the other hand, if you've thrown yourself into the exercises and approached the questions with openness and curiosity, then you may notice some interesting things come up.

Nothing covered here so far is anything new or out of the ordinary, but when you approach a new task with the right attitude, new and astonishing things can happen. Your path will be different from another person's. If you've done plenty of emotional work before, the previous week may have been a good reminder of your principles and a clue of ways you may have been falling short of your goals.

Here are some questions to ask yourself as you consider your progress over this last week:

1. What habits, thought patterns or old cycles do you notice in yourself

that are not serving you or getting in the way of something better?

2. Do you love yourself? Not in the sense that you buy yourself a chocolate once in a while and go for a monthly pedicure, but in the sense that you believe, fundamentally, that you are a good and lovable person?

3. What new habits and lifestyle choices would you like to start incorporating into your daily life?

4. What are you doing every day to support your happiness? What are you doing everyday to undermine your own sense of peace?

5. If your inner dialogue was broadcast onto a radio station, what kind of station would that be?

Day 9

Don't take anything personally

There's a psychological construct called *"locus of control"*, and it can be classified as internal or external. When our locus of control is external, we attribute events to other people, to God, to the world at large. When we have an internal locus of control, we do the opposite: everything that happens in life is because of us and what we do.

Of course, some events in life are down to chance, to forces outside our control, or to other people. And other events are most definitely all our own doing. Seeing what the difference is takes maturity and courage, but this is topic for another day. Nevertheless, people who tend towards depression, anxiety or general dissatisfaction with life tend to share a more internal locus of control.

It's great to take responsibility for the things you do. It's not so great to take responsibility for things that, to put it simply, have nothing to do with you. Let's say you go to a supermarket and as you check out at the till, the cashier is exceptionally rude, and ignores you when you greet her. You leave, feeling a little slighted. What did you do wrong?

Well, chances are, nothing. When it comes to other people's behavior, we often know much much less than we think we do. The most likely explanation is that the cashier was having a bad day or was distracted when she served you. What would be pointless is to sit in the car on your drive home and wonder what you did wrong, stewing over why you're so objectionable, and by the time you pull up to your driveway, you're fuming over how the world is going to the dogs, how people don't have any respect for each other anymore, and how you're sick of being treated like a doormat.

You may carry this irritation with you for the rest of the day, when in fact, it never belonged to you in the first place. You might be surprised to find that if you confronted that cashier the next day, she might not even remember you, let alone admit to treating you poorly on purpose.

If you catch yourself guessing at the motivations of others, stop yourself dead in your tracks and look closely at what information you really have. Is it really about you? Is the interpretation of some situation really correct? Look at the situation from a different perspective and see if it changes things. Try not to assume malevolence when inattention would do fine to explain people's bad or confusing behavior. Be generous. Be willing to say that sometimes people are rude to each other and it has nothing to do with anything.

On the other hand, this same principle goes for compliments too. If someone is especially sweet and kind to you, that's great, but don't automatically assume that it's about you either. If you base your self-worth on how often others compliment and validate you, then you're allowing other people to decide how you feel about yourself. A compliment is simply a reflection of how people see you, and that may or may not be accurate – only you can be the judge of that.

When you have a solid self-concept, when you love yourself and when you act according to your principles and values, the opinions of others (good and bad!) become much less important.

Today's exercise: if someone has been bothering you lately, or there is some unresolved issue with someone else, take a moment to ask how much of it is really your business, and whether you're maybe taking on more than you're really responsible for.

Day 10

Your external environment

We've already explored how a healthy body makes it so much easier to have a healthy mind, but the same is true of your immediate environment. It's difficult to have a light, happy and robust spirit if your environment is dirty, chaotic or constantly getting in your way.

It's easy to focus on the cleanliness of an area, or how organized it is. But is that all? How happy does your space make you? Is it helping you to think positively or doing just the opposite? It's great to de-clutter, clean up and organize your space, not only at work but also at home.

Today, we're also going to look at how an environment can be *supportive*.

Take a quick look at the immediate space you're in. Right now. How does it make you feel? Bored? Irritated? Calm and safe? With a low level of panic? Indifferent? Maybe you have a pile of clutter that you walk past every day that brings your spirit down a little just to look at it. Maybe the color of your walls is depressing you. Maybe you need more plants or natural sunlight in to make your little "nest" feel more homely and welcoming.

Negativity can take many forms, some less expected than others:

- An uncomfortable couch that always makes you ever so slightly grumpy and forces you to slouch.

- Chipped plates and cups that make you feel bad.

- Drafts, cold rooms or dark corners in a house.

- Clutter, piles of dirty clothes, dusty books and "things". These can all represent accompanying mental clutter and dirt. Could you just throw it all out?

- Radio, TV and news stations constantly playing and reminding you of how terrible a place the world is. Do you really want to watch / listen to it?

- Do you have heirlooms or gifts that you only hold onto out of a sense of guilt or obligation?

- Is your house in an unsafe area or too far from where you want to be? Consider your general location and whether really it's suiting your higher values.

A note on "hate-reading" - before you conclude that your immediate environment is just fine, check out one more place you might be harboring negativity: *your mobile phone*. Corrosive and time-wasting online habits can creep up on you and be incredibly difficult to get a handle on. Do you engage in hate reading? Even if you've never heard the term before, you probably already know what this is.

You sit down and check Facebook, and secretly hate the people who are posting pictures of their beach holiday, their children, their stupid complaints and motivational pictures. You go onto Twitter and catch the end of a long, long argument between two of the people you follow. You don't care about why they're arguing; you just get a thrill out of watching it all go down.

Then you check out some of your usual sites, except a good few of them you don't even enjoy reading. They make you angry, or else you deliberately get involved in adversarial comments over an article you never even cared about before you read the title. You read a dumb list "article" on a site you'd be embarrassed to be caught reading, and all the while you're doing it, you're thinking, "ugh I hate this". And yet you do it anyway.

Hate reading is poisonous, for obvious reasons. If you catch yourself doing it, try to figure out what your body and mind might do better with at that moment. Could you read something educational or inspiring? If not, do you even have to be browsing in the first place? A while back, I installed an app that permanently blocked sites I knew upset me from my browser. It was a good move.

Day 11

Practice forgiveness

Yes, another fluffy one!

Forgiveness is one of those things everyone thinks is all well and good, but actually doing it yourself, when it matters, can feel impossible. But it's true what they say: holding onto resentment towards others is like eating poison and expecting them to die. It's a waste of your time and a definite waste of your energy.

Easier said than done, right?

At the core of the unwillingness to forgive others are a few assumptions that, if you look closer, don't really hold water. As we've already seen, jumping to the conclusion that someone who has hurt you has done so deliberately often proves to be incorrect. Getting angry with someone and refusing to forgive their transgressions communicates a few things. It tells your unconscious that your peace of mind is up to somebody else, that they hold the key to your state of mind and you are powerless to do anything about it.

It also communicates that if there is a problem in life, it is always going to be a problem. Being unwilling to forgive means, ironically, that you shut yourself off from the very solutions that would have helped you heal and move on. When you shut down and withhold forgiveness, you don't give yourself or the other person the chance to become better, to learn anything.

Lastly, being unwilling to forgive others often hides a tendency to not want to forgive ourselves. Holding a grudge makes the world look "wrong". It's a weight to carry, and more often than not, the negativity you give a home to will one day be turned onto you.

Of course, we all have our boundaries and occasionally, these boundaries will be violated. Perhaps, the offender hasn't even noticed or doesn't care what they've done. What then? I'm not going to suggest that you take on a Christ-like turn-the-other-cheek approach and meekly treat your abusers like nothing happened. Anger and indignation can be powerful tools to make sure your boundaries are respected.

But at the same time, remember that forgiveness is not for them, it's for *you*. Try to understand where they are coming from. Be patient and understanding with your anger, but open up dialogue and see if some misunderstandings can't be smoothed over. There are no fairy tales in this book - sometimes, bad things happen in life, and forgiveness seems like the furthest thing from your mind. It might pay to think of it like this: you have already suffered at the hands of someone else, don't suffer extra, at your own hands, in holding onto that pain longer than you need to. Extract any useful lessons you can from the episode and then move on.

Today's exercise: bring out all those old resentments and unforgiven trespasses, and see if you can let them go.

Day 12

Play!

Once I was speaking to an old friend who was describing the many years of depression he had endured in the past, and how he was slowly clawing his way out. He said, with an almost stunned look on his face, that the last time he had felt this free and happy was when he was 6 years old.

Sad, isn't it? But he was onto something: when it comes to happiness, children serve as the best example. They live in the moment, they express themselves and their desires freely, they love wholeheartedly and they run around the world with the energy and vitality only matched by adult athletes.

You were a child once, and you experienced this simple, direct joy yourself. Today's exercise is to see if you can remember what that felt like, and unlock it again. Go over old childhood photos if you have them, and try to remember what you were like as a kid.

What excited you nearly half to death? What big dreams did you have? When I remember my childhood, I remember the tantrums, sure, but I also remember spontaneously breaking into dance whenever I felt like it. I remember running up to my mother and giving her a big hug, just because I felt like it. I remember all the adventures and games. What, exactly, is stopping me from doing more of that now?

A good way to nurture happiness in your life is to get in touch with your inner child. Laugh, explore, have fun, make things into a game, let go of overly serious things and be a little mischievous. When you were young, the world seemed like the most enormous, most endlessly fascinating playground. After decades of obligation and disappointments and social conditioning, that spirit got a little squashed. But it's still there!

Today, do whatever the hell you want. The world is still as interesting and fun as it was when you were a child. There are no "have to's" today, only play.

Some ideas:

- Play a prank on someone in your office.

- Buy a waterslide for your back garden - you're a grown up, you're allowed to.

- Organize a game of Frisbee in the park this afternoon with friends.

- Get some props and pose for funny pictures in a photo booth.

- Get busy with crafts, baking, or any hands on activity that you loved as a kid.

- Be a tease! Laugh at yourself and playfully poke fun at others. Tell jokes. You'd be amazed at how interesting the world looks with just a small shift in perspective.

- Play laser tag, do a bungee jump or let a friend dare you to try something you're kind of afraid to try.

- Flirt. Chat up people who look interesting and be fearless about it. You weren't so wary of others as a kid, and it was adorable.

- Sing karaoke, dance, play board games, run outside with the dog or organize an Easter egg hunt. Paint racing stripes on your pet turtle. Why not?

- Go somewhere with no plan, and no itinerary. If you feel like lingering on the beach to hunt for shells, do it. Order something silly and indulgent off the menu. Wear a silly hat in the bath tub. I think you're getting the idea... :)

Day 13

Inviting stillness into your life

I probably don't have to say much to convince you of the value of meditation. Much has been written on how (and why) to meditate, but stillness can be invited into your life in many other, less formal ways. When our minds and hearts are still, it's like the ripples going quiet on the surface of a lake - things are smooth, and we begin to be able to reflect.

A turbulent, busy and overly full mind never stops to think, what am I doing? Why? What's going on here?

So much in the self-help realm is about acquiring. You find happiness, and add it onto your life. You buy *more* products, you hold onto *more* ideas, *more* books, *more* things. Even if you want to lose weight or organize your life, you're encouraged to buy special dieting drugs and tools, or special organizing boxes and the like.

Happiness, though, is also about releasing. It's also about absence, calmness, and tranquility. Some things in life can only be seen when the rest of the mind takes a step back. Every religion in the world recognizes the spiritual and transcendent nature of emptiness, of peace.

The irony is that clinging to an idea of what mediation "should" look like and how best to do it puts your mind in exactly the wrong place. Meditation is not about achievement or striving or goals. So I'm not going to suggest a meditation here, and I'm not going to tell you how to do it.

I am going to invite you to open up tiny pockets of stillness in your life, especially today.

It doesn't matter where you do this or for how long. A little window is a moment where you grab hold of your conscious awareness, and go still for a moment. Pay attention to the moment, and let go. Don't strive, just become aware. You may notice that your body is holding stress, or that you are being mindless in other ways. You may be struck by how beautiful the seagulls actually look as they fly around the dustbin. You may realize that you are feeling sad, and need to nurture yourself a little.

These little moments open up the possibility for deeper self-knowledge, and give you a rich, nuanced control over the very fabric of your experience in this world. Training your brain to be still and receptive prepares it for relaxed, positive emotions. You learn how to let go of life-threatening stress and do something that can be surprisingly hard to do at times: *just be*.

Today's goal: open up a little window. Tomorrow, do it again.

Day 14

Give what you want to receive

Happiness is a paradoxical thing. It sometimes seems that the more you take, the more you need. The more you demand and extract from those around you, the more dissatisfied you feel. I can't say why, but many people instinctively recognize the truth in the principal: to receive, you must give.

When you let go of your own petty desires for a second and become a source of happiness for someone else, something interesting happens. You affirm your power to generate happiness and life, you position yourself in positivity and you literally create positive change in the very world you live in.

Here, I want to make a distinction between kindness, and capital K "Kindness". It might be hard to tell the difference from the outside, but you know the difference, deep down. Consider the act of volunteering for a big, noisy church organized soup kitchen drive and congratulating yourself loudly for being so charitable, so selfless. You pose and posture, feeling so warm and fuzzy that you are now officially a Good Person. Maybe it helps your community, maybe it doesn't, but you feel damn good about yourself and the next time somebody disagrees with you, you hold in the back of your mind the idea that you are secretly superior because, duh, you do so much charity work.

Compare this with another scenario. Your partner comes home from work, flustered after a long and busy day. You are bone tired as well. She is being rude to you, snapping and complaining about every little thing. You love her, so you consciously choose to forgive and forget the behavior. You go out, fetch her a copy of her favorite magazine and a bottle of Champagne, and tell her it's OK, we all have bad days. You don't try to redeem this "favor" later on, and you don't try to guilt her for anything.

Both are varieties of kindness, but the second one is far more likely to effect real change in you, other people and the world around you. Kindness doesn't mean exchanging good behavior for feelings of superiority and vindication. There is no ego in kindness. Sometimes, the kind thing is very difficult to do. Sometimes, the most difficult act of kindness is the one we think of doing the least: being kind to ourselves.

Today, keep your eyes peeled for moments when you can be kind. Flex your muscles of compassion. When you listen to others, really listen without wanting to rush in, without interpreting for them and without giving them "advice". Forgive small insults and inconsiderate behaviors. Choose to brush things off and keep your heart light. Be good to someone not because they "deserve" it, but specifically because they don't, and because there is no "deserve" when it comes to kindness, and because it doesn't matter anyway.

There's a converse to this, too. Being kind also means being receptive to kindness from others. Practice being grateful and gracious for help given to you. Accept compliments without arguing or feeling unworthy. Interpret ambiguous situations positively, instead of assuming the worst of people. Don't be afraid of asking for help and reaching out when you feel overwhelmed. You'd be surprised how willing people actually are to step up and be kind.

Day 15

More reflection

You have reached the end of the first two weeks of your happiness challenge. The time has come again to reflect on your progress. Reflection is great; however this time you're going to examine your progress and come away with real ideas for how to act. Thinking, journaling and meditation are all excellent skills to refine. But happiness is not something you think about; it's something you *do*.

For some people, getting caught up in their heads is a real danger. They talk and think and write about happiness but never give themselves a chance to put any of it into practice. Many self-help gurus might disagree with me here, but I believe that thought alone is not good enough - one has to *act*.

Today, ask yourself again how you are faring in your goal to become happier and more content. If you find snags and places where you're still resistant or still have work to do, then have a closer look. Decide on a course of action to loosen up stuck points and get going again.

You might decide to enroll in a short course, or invite a friend over to have a real conversation about something you're struggling with. You may choose to end a friendship that isn't serving you or initiate contact with someone you've admired from afar. It might be time for a spring clean, time to take a break or time to send out your resume and look for a better job. Whatever it is, identifying the problem is only one half of the solution - the other half is to act.

Day 16

Accepting yourself

*Q**uick*, think of someone who you admire. Maybe a celebrity or other famous person who looks like they have everything all figured out. Now, ask yourself, are they "perfect"? No matter how rich and famous someone is, chances are they have their fair share of haters and critics. Chances are they've had some awful thing happen to them in the past. Chances are they find something they hate about themselves when they look in the mirror in the morning.

My point is that you don't have to be perfect to be happy and successful in life. In fact, many successful people don't overcome their flaws and setbacks, but rather learn to live with them, even capitalizing on them. Think of the comedian who accepts his appearance, makes jokes about it and wins droves of adoring fans because of his honesty and originality. Think of a beautiful model who turns a weird mole or a gap between her teeth or strange hair into her signature, the one thing that makes her stand out from everyone else.

Accepting yourself as you are, right now, is a radical move. I *mean* it. We've already seen how damaging it can be to postpone our own happiness, but when it comes to our appearance or successes and failures in life, it can be tempting to assume that sure, we're lovable ...except for this, that and the other thing.

You know what I'm talking about: someone compliments your weight loss and you say, "yes, well, I still have a long way to go." You wake up in the morning and stare at your reflection, thinking, "I'm happy with the way I look ... as long as I have some foundation on and a bit of mascara. That's all. Oh and some lipstick". You look at your house and think, "this is a great property, I love it. Just a pity about that broken window box."

The message is clear: you can only accept yourself with conditions. The implication is that love is only for those people who are already perfect. *Not true!* There are several tasks for today, many of which will seem easier said than done:

1. Stop comparing yourself to others. Just cut it out, completely. You don't know anything about their lives, and it doesn't matter anyway. It's not a race, and if it were, everyone's running a different race.

2. Stop rushing in to conceal or "fix" vulnerability. Learn to say, "I don't know" or admit when you are afraid or feeling fragile and uncertain. Admit when you're wrong and don't be reluctant to apologize for mistakes.

3. Stop "hedging". Speak clearly and say what you want to say. Stop apologizing for your opinion or your experience. Be open and honest.

4. Express yourself without fear of judgment - whatever your reality is, express it freely.

5. Find those things that make you uniquely you and then stop concealing them - amplify them instead!

Day 17

Get out of your comfort zone

Comfort zones are great. Comfort zones are ... well, *comfortable*. But comfort can also be a bit dangerous. When you are too complacent, stuck in an overly safe routine, your sense of ambition dies. In the brain, doing the same thing over and over looks more or less the same as being depressed. In other words, human beings need to be out there, exploring their worlds and taking risks to be happy.

We are all born with different thresholds for what counts as "exciting" and what's just plain old horrifying and risky. It's all relative. But doing something you've never done before is a very quick and easy way of challenging yourself to be more, to do more. By opening up new perspectives, you refresh your outlook on life and make way for new paths of happiness. You strengthen your character and engage with something zesty and invigorating.

But, I know, it's *scary*.

Then again, all the most exciting and barrier pushing things are scary. That's what makes them so wonderful when you overcome them. It's normal to have fears around certain things, but don't take your fear's word for it. Think it over, is it really so bad? And even if the worst thing happens, is that really so bad?

Buddy up with someone who can give you emotional support and hold you accountable. *Feel the fear and do it anyway.* Maybe it's trying your hand at comedy on an open mic night, maybe it's going into the sauna without feeling shy about being naked, maybe it's rock climbing or jet skiing, maybe it's enrolling for that programming class that you're intimidated by but have been meaning to try for ages. Maybe it's that hot girl at work who you can't summon up the courage to ask out, maybe it's that competition you keep talking yourself out of entering.

If it's a big thing, start small. The exhilaration you feel afterwards may well convince you to do more. Now, take that energy to the rest of your life. What would your life look like if you just did it instead of hanging back out of fear?

Day 18

Learning to reframe

Perspective is everything. The events in our lives are, for the most part, neutral. Things sometimes happen just because they happen. But the way we interpret them depends a lot on our expectations, our conditioning, our goals, our fears and our personalities. It's a good thing to learn how to "put things into perspective", but the question is, whose perspective?

From a certain point of view, all your life problems are completely meaningless. From another point of view, the things you barely notice are cause for celebration. I've always believed that much of the work in changing and improving your life is not even about working on the life itself, but in how you perceive that life!

Today, devote some thought to how to deal with life events like setbacks, mistakes and challenges. The thing about having a worldview is that you're tricked into thinking that it's reality.

But it's not, it's just one of many possible pictures of reality. A worldview is helpful if it stimulates you to be better, and helps you navigate the world and constantly seek out good things. A worldview is less useful if it stunts your actions, makes you unhappy or convinces you of "truths" that just aren't true.

Day 19

Live in the present - intelligently

Somewhere along the line, it became fashionable to try to "live in the moment" and "be mindful". Of course, if you only ever lived in the moment for real, you wouldn't be able to learn from your past mistakes, be creative or make plans for your future. You'd be peaceful, probably, but you'd be more like a goldfish or a squirrel than a switched on, conscious human being.

Humans have developed a great capacity for abstract thought, for planning and for looking into the past and remembering. So, in the most obvious sense, living in the present alone is a poor use of these incredible faculties you were born with.

Without getting too philosophical about it all, I'd like to suggest a way to increase mindfulness, focus and awareness without forcing yourself to "just stop thinking about the past or the future". Today, I'll suggest a way to actually live in the moment - while still being a person who needs to remember their obligations and make plans for retirement.

The way to balance the need to be awake and aware in the present and use our innate mental powers to make smart plans for the future is this: when you do a thing, do it. There's nothing so wrong with worrying about the future, but it becomes a problem if you're absentmindedly missing something really awesome happening right now in front of you.

In the same way, all that inner peace and calm you generate from meditating on the sights and sounds and getting in touch with your bodily sensations means nothing if you can't occasionally make plans for what you'll have for dinner or remember to buy insurance.

The first step is to cut out distractions. Your focus and attention is a limited resource - if you scatter it all over the place, you get nothing done, you stress yourself out and then look back on your life, wondering where all the time went.

So, when you do a thing, do it.

If you are at work staring at your computer screen, being mindful looks like you having the discipline to stop wandering thoughts about what happened last weekend or thinking about what you'll wear to your cousin's wedding next month.

When you are at your cousin's wedding, your attention is on her and the pleasures of spending time with family - being unmindful looks like stressing about work. When you wash your hands, really wash them. Engross yourself in your task, give your focus to what you're doing and do it well. When you sleep, sleep. And when you sit down to make mindful plans about your future, do it.

Learn to strengthen your mind and your will so that you control your thoughts and feelings, not the other way round. So when a thought flitters into your awareness, don't just run after it immediately. Ask yourself, is this relevant right now? Can I do anything about this?

If you are tormented by resentments and regrets from the past, bring that work into the present and stop, look closely and see what you can do, now, to heal and move on. If a thought takes you away from the tasks of the present moment, and never leads to any action, drop it. Similarly, worries about the future can sometimes be extremely useful and appropriate: your mind wants to be careful and plan ahead for the best outcome. If your stress is just endless and doesn't actually lead anywhere: *drop it.*

Once you become comfortable with saying to a thought, "no, you are not necessary and I don't want you" you may indeed notice that you are freer to enjoy the pleasures of the present moment. Your mind will throw up hypotheticals, "what-ifs" and daydreams. Your goal will be to concretize those thoughts and bring them into the present. Here's an example. Let's say you're trying to focus on class one day, but the thought keeps popping up - you're angry with your mother about something and can't let it go. You feel indignant and unsettled about what she did in the past.

Instead of just being some kind of saintly Buddha and letting it "go", you could become curious. Your mind is not happy with the state of things. What action can you take? Perhaps you tell yourself, "this lecture is important so I need to pay attention right now. But I'm realizing that this thing with my mother is not going away. After class I'm going to give her a call and let her know what's on my mind."

Day 20

Challenge your negative thoughts and beliefs

Imagine you had a stupid friend, and every single thing that came out of his mouth, you simply accepted as truth. When he tells you that Chinese astrology only works for Chinese people or that all the chickens at KFC have cancer, you simply nod your head and say, "wow, really? Ok" and believe him.

If you wouldn't believe everything your stupid friend told you, why would you believe everything you tell yourself?

The funny thing about thoughts and beliefs is that they have a way of tricking us into thinking that they are absolute, non-negotiable facts. Your friend might say, "It's true, I swear! I'm not making this up, it's just a fact that mobile phones make your brain cells melt!", but it's not a fact, it's a belief.

The only way to become better and to let go of limiting and unhelpful beliefs is to actually see them in the first place. And the best way to do this is to learn to not take your inner voice's word for it. Byron Katie has an amazing technique for getting around the sometimes silly things we convince ourselves of. Here's the gist of it:

Take any belief you have and ask:

    1. Is it true? (Yes or no. If no, move to 3)

2. Can you absolutely know that it's true? (Yes or no)

3. How do you react, how do you feel, what happens when you believe that thought?

4. Who would you be without the thought?

This series of questions short-circuits unproven, unrealistic thoughts and feelings that hold you back and stunt what you can be and do. Here's an example. You look in the mirror one morning and your inner stupid friend says "you're unlovable and nobody will ever want to marry you". If you're not used to challenging yourself, you might simply say "oh really? Ok" and then go on with your life, utterly miserable given this "truth".

If you don't take your own word for it though, you ask yourself firstly, is it true? Let's say you're being a bit stubborn and say "Yes! I haven't had a relationship in 3 years", well then move onto the next question. Do you absolutely know that? Honestly, you don't. People get married later in life all the time, you were loved in the past and will be again, and in fact several people just told you yesterday how awesome you were. So. How do you react, carrying this thought around? Well, you behave like someone unlovable. You hate yourself. You stop taking risks. Who would you be without this thought? Well, maybe, just maybe, you'd be happier. You'd look in the mirror and say, "hey, I'm alright" and go out into the world, open and receptive to love and adventure.

Today's task: try this formula on your own thought and really challenge that inner stupid friend.

Day 21

Happiness is letting go

To finish off the last day of this happiness challenge, we're going to do a fun exercise. So often, happiness is coded as something you add onto life. Something you buy, someone you meet, something you do or some achievement you reach.

But happiness is also letting go. In your journal, write down every last shred of what you want to let go of. No arguing, not "one day", just let it go, *now*. You have my permission. The world wants you to be happy, and, well … you're in charge. Let it go. Put that pen on paper and write, and don't stop until it's all out. Here are some things that you might like to let go of forever:

- People you don't need or want in your life.

- "Arguing with reality".

- Resentments about exes or what your parents did way back when.

- Inhibitions about what you should or shouldn't do.

- Guilt about what you did long ago.

- Being a people pleaser.

- Regretting what you didn't do long ago.

- Being in control.

- Stressing about things you have no control over.

- Anger at things you can't change.

- Fear about your future.

- Negative self talk.

- Blame.

- The idea that you need to be perfect.

- The idea that you need to be happy all the time.

- Being stubborn about the "right way" to be.

- All your "opinions".

- Your desperation to be accepted by others.

- Money worries.

- Shame about who you are and what you really want.

- Constantly defending yourself.

- Negative people who don't share your values.

- Crippling fear of failure.

- Attachment to end goals and achievements.

- Comparing your life to other people's.

- Expectations, obligations.

- Fear of being alone or fear of being abandoned.

- Low self esteem.

- Excuses!

- Repression and lying to yourself.

- Being shy and not speaking up, not defending your boundaries.

Your list can look like this or be more specific. Maybe a few items on your list will be "little things" like "daily candy" or big things like "my husband". It's all up to you.

Conclusion

I hope that at this point, I have convinced you that when you become aware, when you are courageous and take action to reach your goals each and every day, happiness is not some wishy washy thing, but a reality. Something you grow and nurture every day. Now that you're at the end of the happiness challenge, your task is to find a creative way to incorporate whatever you've learned into the rest of your life.

If you've enjoyed some of the exercises, why not start doing them daily? Hone in on those tasks that you got the most out of and think of a way to bring that energy into your life right now. Whatever you choose to do, my hope is that you believe, at least a little more than you did before, that happiness is a real possibility for you, and that the choice to be content, joyful and focused is and always has been yours.

Your last challenge: it's up to you. Tomorrow, wake up with an open and receptive spirit, and make room in your heart for honesty, creativity and happiness. Design your own 21 days, and don't stop there. The rest of your life is yours for the making. Good luck!

Other 21-Day Challenges you may enjoy!

All challenges are available in Paperback, eBook and Audiobook format

Self-Love

Confidence

Happiness

Mindfulness

Stress Management

Exercise

Weight Loss

Clean Eating

Minimalism

Budgeting

Love Collection – 3 Books: Self-Love, Confidence & Happiness

Complete Collection – 10 Books

www.ingramcontent.com/pod-product-compliance
Lightning Source LLC
LaVergne TN
LVHW031326190726
843493LV00013B/3057